The Future in a
Nutshell
Prophecy for Busy People

By Chris Williams

Writers Exchange E-Publishing
http://www.writers-exchange.com

The Future in a Nutshell
Copyright 2004 Chris Williams
Writers Exchange E-Publishing
PO Box 372
ATHERTON QLD 4883

Published by Writers Exchange E-Publishing
http://www.writers-exchange.com

ISBN **ebook**: 1 920741 82 8
Print: 9781091216037 (Amazon Assigned)

2014 Cover by Josh Shinn, with hourglass figure supplied by
http://commons.wikimedia.org/wiki/User:S_Sepp

The unauthorized reproduction or distribution of this copyrighted work is illegal. Criminal copyright infringement, including infringement without monetary gain, is investigated by the FBI and is punishable by up to 5 (five) years in federal prison and a fine of $250,000.

Names, characters and incidents depicted in this book are products of the author's imagination and are used fictitiously. Any resemblance to actual events, locales, organizations, or persons, living or dead, is entirely coincidental and beyond the intent of the author.

No part of this book may be reproduced or transmitted in any form or any means, electronic or mechanical, including photocopying, recording, or by any information storage and retrieval system, without permission from the publisher.

Scripture taken from the HOLY BIBLE, NEW INTERNATIONAL VERSION. Copyright 1973, 1978, 1984 by International Bible Society. Used by permission of Zondervan Publishing House. All rights reserved.

The "NIV" and "New International Version" trademarks are registered in the United States Patent and Trademark office by International Bible Society. Use of either trademark requires permission of the International Bible Society.

All Bible verses mentioned in the book, but not written in full, can be found in full at the back of the book; these have all been taken from the King James Version.

Table of Contents

Introduction

This book was written because I believe it's important for everybody to know what the Bible says about the future. There are many fine books about Bible prophecy, but many are long, and use theological language that often escapes the average, faithful member of our Bible-believing churches. Busy living life, and reluctant to add any thing else to an already filled plate, many believers shy away from any kind of extensive study of Eschatology. The thought of climbing "Mount Prophecy" is daunting, and most decline the challenge, to leave the study of things to come to the "experts" and "scholars".

The Future in a Nutshell is an attempt to acquaint these reluctant laypersons with some of the basic tenets of Biblical Eschatology. Complex theological language has been avoided whenever possible, and is explained when its use can't be avoided. Obviously, a work this short couldn't possibly be a complete look at God's plans for the future. But it does cover some of the basics, and is a useful overview of what the Bible says about the future. It is simple and brief and can be easily "plugged into" the busy lives of almost everyone.

I hope you are blessed by *The Future in a Nutshell,* and find it useful. I also pray that the Lord is pleased with my efforts, and uses this little book to draw people closer to Himself.

Chris Williams

Chapter One
What's Going to Happen?

The world can be a scary place. The streets of many of our cities and towns aren't safe, horrible diseases that have no cure are in the news, and terrorists have threatened the lives of anyone who disagrees with their beliefs. Mothers and fathers are getting divorced in record numbers, leaving millions of sad and confused children with hurts they'll carry for the rest of their lives. Things seem to be out of control. What's going to happen in the days and years ahead?

Sometimes it's hard to admit that we're scared and have questions about the future. Nobody wants to seem "stupid", so most of us keep our questions to ourselves. But people have wondered about the future for thousands of years. Even the followers of Jesus Christ wanted some "inside" information:

"Tell us," they said, "when will this happen, and what will be the sign of your coming and the end of the age?"
- Matthew 24:3b

Notice that Jesus didn't make fun of His followers when they asked questions about the future. Instead, He gave them straight answers. To find out what He said, get a Bible and turn to Matthew, chapter 24, verses 4 through 22. (It would be an excellent idea to keep a Bible nearby as you read this book. Look up the verses for yourself. Don't just take my word for everything!)

Here's a summary of what Jesus said in Matthew 24: 4-22:

In the "last days" liars will appear, teaching things that contradict God's teachings in the Bible. Some will even claim to be sent from God to save the world.

As time goes on, wars and the threat of wars will increase.

The lack of food in many countries will get worse and worse, with millions dying from hunger.

In the future, earthquakes will become a major problem all over the world. It's true that earthquakes have been with us from the beginning of time, but in the "last days", there will be a lot more of them!

In the future, widespread epidemics of deadly diseases will plague the world.

Many Christians will suffer greatly for following Jesus, some even being killed for their faith.

God won't let mankind completely destroy the earth or wipe out the human race.

God wants to teach us about the future, too. Instead of sitting down with us on a mountain (like He did in Matthew 24), these days He speaks to us through the words of the Bible. Go to the Bible with an open mind and heart, and the Lord will show you many things. Jesus promised:

Ask and it shall be given you; seek, and ye shall find, Knock, and it shall be opened unto you.
Matthew 24:7 KJV

The Heavenly Father delights in giving answers from His Word. But He's not going to drop this stuff down "special delivery" without any effort on our part. We need to "knock" and "seek", which simply means we need to "just do it" by opening up the Bible and reading it, and sincerely praying about what we read.

And as you read, pray and think, keep the following Bible verse in mind:

All Scripture is God-breathed and is useful for teaching, rebuking, correcting and training in righteousness.
2 Timothy 3:16

Don't forget this verse when you come across confusing parts of the Bible. God gave us the scripture; He knows what the "tricky" verses mean. If you give it a sincere and honest try, the Lord promises to help you understand (Proverbs 2:6).

The key to understanding what the Bible says about the future is to find out as much as you can about Jesus Christ. He is at the center of everything God plans to do. Some things in the Bible won't seem so incredible or confusing when you discover who He really is. The picture will get clearer if you focus on Jesus Christ.

The Bible says that Jesus is the Son of God (Matthew 17:5). This is very important to remember, as God told the Old Testament writers and readers that the Son is equal to the Heavenly Father in every way (Isaiah 9:6). When Jesus claimed to be God's Son in Matthew, Chapter 10, the religious leaders became very angry. As a matter of fact, they picked up stones to throw at Him. They wanted Him to die! Jesus said:

I have shown you many great miracles from the Father. For which of these do you stone Me?
Matthew 10:32

For just a regular person to claim to be God is a terrible sin. When Jesus claimed to be God's Son, they thought He was absolutely and completely out of line. They didn't accept Him, and accused Jesus of blasphemy, which is saying and/or doing something totally outrageous against God.

But Jesus Christ was not just "a regular person". The Bible teaches that Jesus was, indeed, the Son of God, and offers the following proofs:

Jesus CREATED everything (John1:3). Who else but God could have done that?

Jesus KNOWS everything (Colossians 2:3). There are some super smart people, but only God knows everything.

Jesus is SINLESS (2 Corinthians 5:21). This means that Jesus Christ never did anything wrong or broke any of God's laws, rules or commandments, and never will.

Jesus CONTROLS NATURE (Matthew 8:23-27). No one on Earth has this power.

Jesus FORGIVES our sins (Matthew 9:1-8). Only God can forgive sin.

Jesus let people WORSHIP Him (Revelation 5:11-14). To worship anyone or anything but God is blasphemy. A lot of people who aren't Christians like to say that, even though they're not believers, they think that Jesus was a very good man, perhaps the best who ever lived.

If Jesus wasn't really God, and allowed anyone, anywhere to worship Him, then He wasn't a very good man. He wasn't even a good man. Any mere man who accepts the worship that is due only to God, is a very wicked person and the worst kind of blasphemer.

So, if you're tempted to think that Jesus was a good man, but aren't willing to believe in Him, keep in mind that

He accepted worship. In Exodus 20:3, God said He would never accept any other gods before Him!

Jesus has POWER OVER DEATH (John 11: 1-54). He raised people from the dead, and death itself couldn't keep Him in the grave after He was killed by His enemies (Matthew 28:6-7).

Finally, don't forget that Jesus Himself claimed to be God (John 10:30-33).

"Wait a minute!" someone might say. "I thought God was a spirit. Jesus was born a baby in Bethlehem. Doesn't that make Him just a human being?"

That's an excellent question. The answer is that Jesus Christ is very special, and unlike any person who ever lived. As God's Son, He has always existed in spirit. He had no spiritual beginning (Isaiah 9:6, Micah 5:2). Because He loved us, Jesus came to Earth and died for our sins (Hebrews 2: 9-10). It was a mission He wasn't forced to take:

> *The reason My Father loves Me is that I lay down My life - only to take it up again. No one takes it from Me, but I lay it down of My own accord...*
> John 10: 17, 18A

At no time when Jesus was on earth did He stop being God. He chose to appear in human form and live among mankind. It's hard to understand and a lot harder to explain, but it's a fact that Jesus Christ perfectly blended the Spirit of God and a sinless human body and life. Jesus performed many miracles during His years on earth; these incredible events were meant to show the world that He was God's Son (John 10:38). His enemies ignored the evidence, and pushed to have Him killed.

Talking about God's plans for the future is not supposed to be an exercise in cramming a bunch of Bible facts into our heads. It's supposed to bring us closer to a real Person who lives and loves us all very much. This person is Jesus Christ, and He has promised to return to Earth someday (Matthew 24:44).

This discussion is about many of the important things that will happen before, during and after that special day. That's why finding out as much as we can about Jesus Christ is the key; His return is at the center of God's plans for the future.

Chapter Two
"What Happens When I Die?"

ave you ever wondered what REALLY happens when you die? Some people believe our spirits fall into a long, deep sleep, and will someday be awakened on Resurrection Day. Another school of thought is that when a Christian dies, they are transported outside of time straight to the resurrection so that it feels instantaneous for them, even though their bodies may have been "asleep" in the grave for a long time. Others think this life is all there is, and when we die, that's it, we're completely gone, and cease to exist in any way (except for the lifeless body we leave behind). Some religions says that we come back as another person, animal or bug. Still others think that everyone goes to a wonderful place called Heaven when we die, regardless of what we did in this life.

According to the Bible, these ideas are wrong. Take a look at Luke, chapter 16, verses 19-23:

There was a rich man who was dressed in purple and fine linen and lived in luxury every day. At his gate was laid a beggar named Lazarus, covered with sores and longing to eat what fell from the rich man's table. Even the dogs came and licked his sores.

The time came when the beggar died and the angels carried him to Abraham's side. The rich man also died and was

> *buried. In Hell, where he was in torment, he looked up*
> *and saw Abraham far away, with Lazarus by his side.*

Notice that when Lazarus and the rich man died, their spirits continued to live. They were alert and knew what was going on around them. Also, they ended up in two different places; Lazarus joined Abraham in Heaven, and the rich man went to Hell. The Bible says that everyone dies once (Hebrews 9:27), and each of us make the choice where we go when we die:

> *This day I call Heaven and Earth as witnesses against you that I*
> *have set before you life and death, blessings and curses. Now choose life,*
> *so that you and your children may live.*
> Deuteronomy 30:19

The way to "choose life" is to believe in Jesus Christ and turn your life over to Him. There are many places in the Bible where it is shown that faith in Jesus is the only way to Heaven, including John 14:6, John 3:16, and Romans 10:9-10.

Many people don't like to hear this kind of thing. They think that God is too loving and kind to send anybody to a place of punishment forever. But in Matthew 25:41, Jesus warned us about a place of "eternal fire" where many would go when they die.

"I see," you might say. "You either go to Heaven or Hell when you die. And that's it, right?"

Well, that's it until something incredible happens called the First Resurrection. The Bible is filled with details about times when God displayed His mighty power and performed fantastic deeds called "miracles". A few examples include the time God sent a flood that covered the whole earth (Genesis 7:11), the day the Lord took care of a man who was swallowed whole by a giant fish (Jonah 2:10), and when God protected a fellow who was forced to spend the night in a den of hungry lions (Daniel 6:19-22).

One of God's greatest miracles is yet to come, and it's called "The First Resurrection". *Webster's Dictionary* says the word "resurrection" means "the act of rising from the dead". In other words, people who are dead are brought back to life by some sort of outside force. The Bible teaches that this force is actually a person, and that person is God.

Someday, God is going to raise from the dead everyone who ever believed and trusted in Jesus as the only way to Heaven. That group will include many who lived hundreds of years before Jesus was born, and who believed God's promises in the Old Testament. A man named Job lived a long, long time before Jesus came to Earth, but still trusted Him:

> *I know that my Redeemer lives, and that in the*
> *end He will stand upon the Earth.*
> Job 19:25

In a split second, believers raised from the dead will be given new bodies and rejoined with their spirits (I Thessalonians 4:16). An instant later, believers who are alive when Jesus comes back will experience something incredible. In the first letter to the Thessalonians, the Apostle Paul says that God will supernaturally change their bodies, and then:

> *...we who are still alive and are left will be caught up together*
> *with them in the clouds to meet the Lord in the air.*
> *And so we will be with the Lord forever.*

1 Thessalonians 4:17

You need to notice something very important here; *there will be a group of Christians who never die!* This part of the First Resurrection is called *The Rapture* by Bible teachers. The word "rapture" is from the Latin language, and means "a snatching away". Someday, the God of heaven is going to "snatch" all the people who believe in Him out of this world.

Everyone who is raised or "raptured" at this time will be like Jesus (I John 3:2), in that they won't be able to sin and will never feel pain or get sick again. They will be invited to a big celebration called "The Wedding Supper of the Lamb" (Revelation 19:7-9). At this celebration, believers will praise Jesus and enjoy being in His presence. At some point during the celebration, Jesus will give out rewards for those who served Him when they lived on earth (2 Corinthians 9:10). Some will receive large rewards, some less, and still others, who trusted Jesus but did little or nothing for Him, will get nothing but the privilege of living in Heaven (I Corinthians 3:14-15), which isn't such a bad reward all by itself!

All those who served Jesus Christ, including the ones who received big rewards, will realize that their good deeds didn't save them. The Bible says we're saved by faith and not by our works (Ephesians 2:8-10). In deep appreciation for His blessings and love, all believers will toss their rewards at Jesus' feet (Revelation 4:10). Gladly, they will cry out:

You are worthy, O Lord,
To receive glory and honor and power;
For you created all things,
And by Your will they exist and were created.

11

Revelation 4:11

The First Resurrection will be a wonderful time for all who experience it!

The Bible talks about ANOTHER resurrection. It's called "The Second Resurrection", and will be for everyone who has rejected God and His Son, Jesus Christ. It is definitely not the one you want to be a part of! More on that sad event later.

Keep reading!

Chapter Three
The Coming World-Wide Holocaust

To many people, the Rapture sounds like the plot of a far-out sci-fi movie, complete with plenty of computer-generated special effects. If is seems strange to you, and pretty unbelievable, you need to realize that GOD CAN DO ANYTHING HE CHOOSES TO DO! In Genesis 17:1 (and many other places), God is described as being "Almighty". This means He is all-powerful, and can do anything He wants to do. The only things God can't do are things that would go against who and what He is. For example, God can't lie (Hebrews 6:18) or do anything wrong or sinful (I John 3:9).

For the all-powerful God, a miracle like the Rapture will be "no sweat". And it will be a real attention-getter! The sudden disappearance of millions of believers in such a visible way will frighten millions upon millions left here on Earth. Many will turn to the Bible for an explanation, and many will trust Jesus to save them from an "afterlife" far from God and in terrible pain (Revelation 7:9-14). The following Bible verse will be just as true after the Rapture as it is today:

*For God so loved the world that He gave His one and only
Son, that whoever believes in Him shall not perish
but have eternal life.*
John 3:16

The Bible calls this period of time following the Rapture the "Tribulation" (Matthew 24:21). Earth will be rocked with massive earthquakes, deadly diseases, the bloodiest war of all time, and other terrible events. Jesus describes that dark time thusly:

...those will be days of distress unequaled from the beginning, when God created the world, until now - and never to be equaled again.

Earth has seen plenty of bad times. Wars, hunger, sickness, and disasters have been with us for thousands of years. But according to the Bible, it will be the worst period of time in mankind's history.

In the past, some countries escaped destruction experienced by other parts of the world. For example, during World War II, no U.S. city was bombed by enemy planes, while places like London, Berlin and Hiroshima suffered greatly from attack. This will not be the case during the Tribulation. Jesus described that period of time as being:

...the hour of trial that is going to come upon the whole world to test those who live on Earth.
Revelation 3:10B

In other words, the Tribulation will hit the entire world. No continent, land or people will escape.

The Tribulation will also be different in several other ways. Revelation, chapter 16 says that people living at that time will experience:

a) Painful sores (verse 2) - sores have been around for a long time, but we've never seen the world-wide epidemic of sores that will strike countless millions of people who reject God and His Son.

b) Vast areas of the world's seas becoming like blood, killing everything in them (verse 3) - pollution is a problem, but nothing even CLOSE to this has ever plagued the world's oceans.

c) Rivers and other water sources turning to blood (verse 4) - man needs water to survive. During the Tribulation, fresh water will all but disappear from the face of the Earth.

d) A battle involving ALL the armies of the world (verses 13-14) - even during World Wars I and II, no battles involved every single army on Earth.

e) A massive earthquake shaking the entire world (verses 18-19) - this will be in addition to the numerous earthquakes that Jesus said would occur during this period of time.

f) Giant, 100 pound hailstones falling from the sky (verses 20 - 21) - there have been some very intense hail storms over the centuries, but nothing involving 100 pound hailstones! Think of the destruction that will cause!

Are you starting to get the idea that the Tribulation is going to be a lot more than just a bunch of everyday problems?

As these horrible events begin to hit the earth, mankind will be looking for someone to lead them out of the mess they're in. In desperation, they will turn to a man who will appear, at first, to be a great man of peace. But Jesus Christ is the true "Prince of Peace", and this coming world leader will only make things much worse. More about him in the next chapter.

Chapter Four
The Ultimate Bad Guy

During the coming Tribulation, the vast majority of the world's population will reject Jesus, and will choose instead to follow the most evil person of all time.

Two names the Bible gives this wicked person are the Antichrist (I John 2:18) and the Beast (Revelation 13:1). The name "Beast" is meant to be a word picture. He won't actually be an animal, but he will be fierce and dangerous like a wild beast. The word "Antichrist" means "against Christ"; this means he will fight against Jesus, God and everything in the Bible. Many leaders have hated Jesus throughout history, but the Antichrist will be the champion of them all!

Antichrist will have a partner in his schemes to rule the world. The Bible calls this person another beast (Revelation 13:11) and the False Prophet (Revelation 20:10). He will perform miracles, and will urge people not just to follow the Antichrist, but to worship him (Revelation 13:14). Where will the False Prophet get his power? 2 Thessalonians 2:9 says the source will be God's ancient arch-enemy:

> *The coming of the lawless one will be in accordance with the work of Satan*
> *displayed in all kinds of counterfeit miracles, signs and wonders.*

Not all miracles come from God. Satan has power, too, and he will use it to make the Antichrist look like the answer to the world's problems. People like to be entertained. Instead of trusting God and reading the Bible, most would rather turn off their brains. Believing in a miracle we have just seen isn't hard, and Satan will use mankind's spiritual laziness to get them excited about the Antichrist.

Real faith doesn't depend on signs, wonders and miracles. Jesus said, "Blessed are those who have not seen and yet have believed." (John 20:29).

God does have the power to do miracles, but He's not going to drop them down to us like rain to keep us believing in Him. According to Hebrews 11:1, that's not what faith is all about:

Now faith is the substance of things hoped for,
the evidence of things not seen.

During the Tribulation, millions will reject true faith, and will put their trust in the Antichrist and his miracle-working partner, the False Prophet. While most of the world worships him, the Antichrist will say terrible things against the God of Heaven. As-a-matter-of-fact, he will claim to be greater than God Himself! (Daniel 11:36-37).

Back in 1963, US President John F. Kennedy was shot and killed in Dallas, Texas. Imagine what would have happened if, a couple days after his death, President Kennedy got out of his coffin and announced he needed to get back to work. Surely, such an event would have shaken the entire world. During the Tribulation, Satan will attempt to counterfeit just such an event. Check out Revelation 13:3:

One of the heads of the beast seemed to have had a fatal wound,
But the fatal wound had been healed.
The whole world was astonished and followed the beast.

Read that verse again slowly. The Antichrist is going to appear to die, but will come back to life. Notice the word "seemed"; this verse doesn't say that the Antichrist will actually die, only that he will seem to die. People will be amazed and will gladly follow someone who seems to have power over death. Antichrist's power will appear to have come from Heaven, and millions will worship him.

This evil man will be a great military leader. Every country that comes against Antichrist's armies will be defeated. He will be so successful on the battlefield that his opponents will wonder - "who can make war against him?" (Revelation 13:4). For a while, the Antichrist will be unbeatable. He will bring his enemies under control, and a brief period of peace will descend upon a war-sick world. But it won't last:

While people are saying, peace and safety
Destruction will come on them suddenly,
as labor pains on a pregnant woman,
and they will not escape.
I Thessalonians 5:3

God has a plan for this world, and the Antichrist will be powerless to stop it! The peace will soon be shattered (Revelation 6:8), and the Lord will turn the sun black, the moon red, and will send meteors to pound the earth (Revelation 6:12). Escape will be impossible.

With the world in confusion, Antichrist will take control of the world's money and business. Every man, woman and child will be forced to:

Receive a mark on his right hand or on his forehead,
so that no one could buy or sell unless he had the mark,

19

which is the name of the beast or the number of his name; his number is 666.
Revelation 13:16-17, 18B

The Bible doesn't tell us exactly how he's going to do it, but Antichrist is going require everyone on Earth to take the number "666" in order to survive. Without the number, you will not be able to purchase necessities like food and clothing, or even run a business. Even today, with cards and numbers being used for almost everything we do, it's easy to see how Antichrist could pull off such a world-wide plan. Following the September 11, 2001 terrorist attacks, there was a call in the United States to give everyone an ID card. During the Tribulation, Antichrist will require some sort of world-wide ID system. The Bible says that instead of cards being used, this number will be somehow implanted onto the forehead or on the right hand (Revelation 13:16). It will look like a great idea, but whoever takes Antichrist's number will be doomed:

If anyone worships the beast and his image, and receives his mark...he
himself shall also drink of the wine of the wrath of God, which is poured
out full strength into the cup of His indignation. He shall be tormented
with fire and brimstone...
Revelation 14:9B, 10A

Those true believers in Jesus Christ who trusted him after the Rapture will not take the number of the Beast. Many will be killed, or will die for their faithfulness to God's Son (Revelation 7:14B-17, 13:15).

As you can see, the book of Revelation has a lot to tell us about the future. This book often scares or confuses people, and many prefer not to think about it. It is filled with word pictures and mysterious sayings, and is sometimes hard to understand. But understanding at least part of the last book of the Bible is not impossible.

Chapter Five
More About the Book of Revelation

Despite what some people think, not everything in Revelation is hard to understand. Some verses and teachings are "no brainers". Many don't know this because they've come across some of the tricky parts in the past, became frustrated, and gave up on the whole book. If you get a grip on the easier verses, it will help you understand many of the harder ones.

The first verse of Revelation gives us the key to the rest of the book. It says it is "the Revelation of Jesus Christ". Chapters 1 through 22 "reveal" much about Jesus Christ and what will happen before and after He returns to Earth. We see God finally punishing the wicked for their sins, and for rejecting His Son. In Heaven, there is a wonderful scene of angels and believers worshipping Jesus. Toward the end of the book, we read about the day Christ will lead a heavenly army to Earth to set up a fantastic kingdom. And those are just some of the highlights!

Take a look at Revelation 1:7. It's a good example of something that's not too hard to understand:

Look, He is coming with the clouds, and every eye will see Him, even those who pierced Him; and all the peoples of the earth will mourn because of Him. So shall it be! Amen.

You don't need a Bible college degree to understand that the verse teaches:

a) Jesus will come back to Earth.

b) When He does, the whole world will see Him.

c) People will be very unhappy about His return.

Revelation 7:9-17 describes a giant worship service in Heaven. Verse 14 says that the worshippers had died during the Tribulation. In other words, the Lord will continue to have mercy on individuals who turn to Him after the First Resurrection. It's not God's wish that any person spend eternity in Hell (2 Peter 3:9).

Although God loves unbelievers, He forces no one to believe in Him. Everyone has a free choice to accept or reject Jesus as personal Savior (Romans 10:9-11). During the Tribulation, God will shake the Earth in one last attempt to get mankind's attention. According to Revelation 9:20-21, many will not "get the hint", and will continue to reject Jesus Christ. Instead, they will choose:

- to worship false gods,

- to make money and riches the most important things in their lives,

- to contact evil spirits instead of the true God,

- to break God's rules about sex as given in the Bible,

- to steal whatever they want, whenever they think they can "get away with it".

God will send two special messengers to warn unbelievers to turn to Him before it's too late. They will boldly speak God's word, and will do "eye popping" miracles to get the world's attention:

These men have power to shut up the sky so that it will not rain during the time they are prophesying: and they have power to turn waters into blood and to strike the earth with every kind of plague as often

as they want.
Revelation 11:6

Their goal won't be to entertain; they will call people to believe in Jesus Christ. Some will accept God's gift of salvation, but the rest will hate these messengers. The Lord will protect them until their job is done, and then He will allow them to be killed by the Antichrist (Revelation 11:7). The world will celebrate their deaths and for three and a half days:

Every people, tribe, language and nation will
gaze on their bodies and refuse them burial.
Revelation 11:9B

When Revelation was written about 2,000 years ago, this prophecy (God's promise of a future event) seemed impossible. Long before the invention of TV, no one could imagine the entire world being able to look at the bodies of these two messengers at the same time. In the 21st century, we have satellites that beam pictures all over the Earth. It's possible to watch a sporting event or a breaking news story thousands of miles away *as it happens!* Technology will bring the event spoken of in Revelation 11:9 to TV sets all over the world.

For hundreds of years, the prophecy in Revelation 13:16-18 about the "mark of the Beast" seemed like a fairy tale. Controlling the world's money supply with just a number sounded impossible. But, as mentioned in the last chapter, we now have numbers for just about everything. The thought of an evil ruler using a number to control the world's population is not so far-fetched, after all. Today, the basic truth about Revelation 13:16-18 can be understood by nearly everybody who takes time to read the verses.

Here's a short list of verses to look up in Revelation that you won't need a degree in theology to understand. Get a Bible and check them out:

1:3 - God promises a special blessing to everyone who reads Revelation.

22:7 - ANOTHER blessing promised for reading and studying Revelation. It's the only book of the Bible with two promises of blessing for those who read it. God knows Revelation has hard parts, and offers "extra credit" to those who try to understand it.

16:15-17 - People will try to hide and escape from the awful events of the Tribulation. Verse 15 also teaches that the world will be surprised by the return of Jesus.

20:4 - Someday, Jesus Christ will set up a wonderful 1,000 year kingdom here on earth.

20:10, 15 - Satan, the Antichrist, the False Prophet, and unbelievers of all ages will end up in a place called "The Lake of Fire", forever.

22:17 - The cost of becoming a believer in Jesus.

3:20 - Jesus wants to be part of our lives and is willing to wait for us to invite Him in.

10:1-4 - There are some things God plans to do during the Tribulation that aren't mentioned in Revelation (or the rest of the Bible)!

21:1 - God plans on creating a new Heaven and a new Earth. The old Heaven will be history, and this Earth will be "toast" (2 Peter 3:10).

9:16 - Jesus Christ was, is, and will be the greatest King of all time.

Details about the kingdom to be ruled by the "King of Kings and Lord of Lords" are coming up in the next chapter!

Chapter Six
Real Peace

Thinking about the Tribulation can be depressing. Destruction, war and death are not cheerful topics. But reading about what happens AFTER those terrible years is exciting!

Jesus is coming to rule the world (Revelation 20:4). People won't fight, squabble or kill each other. Bombs and bullets will be a thing of the past, as all weapons will be made into tools to help people (Isaiah 2:4).

Even the wild animals will live at peace:

The wolf and the lamb will feed together,
and the lion will eat straw like the ox,
but dust will be the serpent's food.
They will neither harm nor destroy...
Isaiah 65:25

The capitol city of the coming kingdom will be Jerusalem (Isaiah 2:1-3).

At that time, the world will see...

Widespread joy and happiness (Isaiah 35:10). This era of good feeling will stretch around the globe, and will be felt in all countries.

Unbelievable riches (Micah 4:4a). Everybody will have what they need. Because weapons will no longer be needed, there will be a lot more money around to use for good.

Complete safety (Micah 4:4b). Jesus will be in absolute control, and will protect the citizens of His kingdom.

Extremely long human lives (Isaiah 65:20). People will live a lot longer than they do now. With sin under control, there will be a lot less sickness and diseases to plague the human race. With more money to use, those who do get sick will have no problem getting the medicine they need.

Worship of King Jesus, God's Son, face-to-face (Revelation 22:4). Everyone on Earth will worship Jesus (Isaiah 11:9).

Who will populate this fantastic kingdom? Believers who trusted Jesus during the horrors of the Tribulation and survived, babies born during and after the Tribulation, and believers of all ages who returned with Christ from Heaven to defeat the Antichrist.

The vast majority of citizens will gladly follow Jesus. Their hearts will be filled with thankfulness, and they'll want to worship Him. The countries of the world will be filled with true believers (Psalm 72:17c). If someone disobeys God's laws, they will be dealt with quickly (Psalm 2:9). No problem will be allowed to get out-of-hand.

However, God doesn't control people like puppets. He never forces anyone to believe in His Son. During the Kingdom, some will ACT like they are followers of Jesus. Towards the end of what Bible teachers call the "Kingdom Age", Satan will be set loose, and will try to cause trouble again. Because the human heart won't be perfect, many will listen to Satan's lies, and will follow him (Revelation 20:7-8). The Lord won't wait to deal with this situation. Immediately, He will send fire down from Heaven to wipe out these rebels (Revelation 20:9). Satan will be thrown into the Lake of Fire, joining Antichrist and the False Prophet forever (Revelation 20:10).

Earlier, we talked about the First Resurrection and the Rapture. At that time, the bodies of believers of all ages who had passed away will be raised to rejoin their spirits. Also, believers alive at that time will be supernaturally changed, and both groups will soar up to meet Jesus in the clouds.

Unbelievers of all ages face a resurrection, too. At the end of the Kingdom Age, the bodies of unbelievers will be raised and rejoined with their spirits. This is what Bible teachers call "the Second Resurrection". Jesus will sit on a great, white throne (Revelation 20:11), and will examine everything unbelievers did when they lived on Earth. So-called good and bad deeds will be judged (Revelation 20:13). When Jesus is finished, He will say "not enough!" to those who hope their good works outweigh the bad things they did in this life.

Why?

Galatians 3:10-11 says that no one can do enough good things to earn their way into Heaven. Salvation from spending forever apart from God is in trusting Jesus Christ as Savior. Even if a person could live a nearly perfect life, just one sin would keep them out of Heaven. Everyone who stands before Jesus at the "great, white throne" is guilty of that one sin - rejecting Him as Savior (Romans 10:9-11).

Christ rejecters will be thrown into the awful lake of fire with no hope of escape (Revelation 20:15).

After the kingdom and the great, white throne judgment, the next thing on God's agenda is found in 2 Peter 3:10:

The heavens will disappear with a roar;
the elements will be destroyed by fire,
and everything in it will be laid bare.

After destroying the old, God will present a new Heaven and a new Earth (Revelation 21:1). The new Earth will be much better than the old; all the bad things that ever existed will be gone forever. There will be no tears, death or pain (Revelation 21:23). There will be no need for sun, moon, lights and lamps.

How bright is God's glory? It can be blinding, as Saul of Tarsus discovered:

> *As he neared Damascus on his journey,*
> *suddenly a light from heaven flashed around him...*
> *For three days he was blind, and did not eat or drink anything.*
> Acts 9:3, 9

Luke 9:20 describes God's glory as being "as bright as a flash of lightening". God has enough light in His very being to supply all light needs forever. Electric bills will be a thing of the past!

Bible teachers call this period "the Eternal State", meaning it will last forever. It will be a busy and active time. Many will work in government, as the nations of the new Earth will need leaders (Revelation 22:5, Matthew 25: 14-23). But unlike in the past, these governments will be perfect, and the world will be a happy place (Isaiah 65:17-25).

Worship and praise of God and His Son will be the main activity (Revelation 21:24). Citizens will be able to look into Christ's face, and tell Him how much they love Him (Revelation 22:4). No doubt, Jesus will tell them how much He loves them, too. Everyone will be willing and happy servants to God, ready to do whatever He desires (Revelation 22:2-3).

If you're a believer in Jesus, these promises should fill you with hope for the future (Titus 2:13). If you're not trusting Jesus Christ, thinking about these things are probably scary and confusing. You might even be wondering, what makes Christians so special? How come they get to be with God? They're not better than I am! Read the next chapter to find out what makes believers in Jesus Christ different from those who aren't following Him.

Chapter Seven
Back to the Future in Genesis

The Bible tells us that the human race began in a beautiful place called Eden (Genesis 1:27). The first two people, Adam and Eve, had everything they needed. God gave them almost everything in Eden to use and enjoy. There was only one thing they weren't allowed to do:

But of the tree of the knowledge of good and evil,
you shall not eat, for in the day you eat of it you shall surely die.
Genesis 2:17

Unfortunately, Adam and Eve disobeyed God's command, and ate fruit from that one "off-limits" tree (Genesis 3:6). Before that day, their spirits were clean and pure. They could have lived in Eden forever, happy and in perfect health. When they disobeyed the Lord, their spirits were ruined, and someday their bodies would have to die (Genesis 2:17, 3:19).

Because Adam and Eve were the very first people, the whole human race is related to them. Everybody "inherits" their spiritual problem:

Therefore, just as through one man sin entered
the world and death through sin, and thus death
spread to all men, because all sinned-
Romans 5:12

In other words, we're all like "Papa" Adam and "Mama" Eve! Because we have inherited ruined spirits, we do things that displease God (Romans 7:19). We can't help ourselves; it's as natural as breathing (Ephesians 2:3).

It's true that not everybody is a terrible criminal. Some people are quite nice and are willing to help others. Some, like Mother Teresa, even do great things for the human race. The problem is that God is totally pure and clean, unable to do anything wrong, and won't allow anything spiritually dirty near Him (Revelation 21:27). Even if it was possible to live your whole life and do just one thing wrong, that one thing (called "sin" in the Bible) would keep you out of Heaven! Read James 2:10:

For whoever shall keep the whole law, and yet stumble in one point, he is guilty of all.

This means that God is absolutely holy (spiritually pure), and hates even one sin. Humans like to compare each other; it makes us feel better when we see someone who acts worse than we do. But compared to God, all humans look dirty and rotten, even "good" people. This includes very religious people who often do a pretty good job of keeping God's laws. Because of God's holiness, they're in no better shape than the worst person who has broken all of God's commandments. Read Psalm 14:2, 3:

The Lord looks down from heaven upon the children of men, to see if there are any who understand, who seek after God. They have all turned aside, they have together become corrupt; There is none who does good, No, not one.

This description of the human race is based on God's standard of "good", which is absolute perfection. No one approaches the absolute goodness of God. We don't even come close. IF GOD ALLOWED ONE DIRTY HUMAN SPIRIT TO LIVE IN HEAVEN, IT WOULD RUIN THE PLACE!

This news sounds totally depressing, but God has provided a way to meet His standard of perfection. He loves people and doesn't want to see anybody end up in the lake of fire (2 Peter 3:9). So, He sent Jesus Christ to die for us on the cross (John 3:16). As God's Son, Jesus is perfect, and is the only one who could have "paid our bill" to God.

Every real Christian, who ever lived, deserves to spend eternity apart from God, but Jesus Christ took their place. They are not "saved" because they're better than other people or belong to a certain religious group. True believers are believers because they've accepted God's gift; they don't deserve it, and could never do enough to earn it (Ephesians 2:8-10). This gift is the opportunity to trust Jesus Christ as Savior (Romans 10:9-11).

At the moment a person believes in Jesus, God's Holy Spirit comes to live inside of him (2 Corinthians 6:16). Also, the new believers' own spirit comes to life again:

Jesus answered and said to him,
"Most assuredly, I say to you,
unless one is born again, he cannot
see the kingdom of God.
John 3:3

Being "born again" is how the Bible describes the difference between a real Christian and someone who just SAYS they're a believer.

When a person becomes a Christian, the Holy Spirit will help him to obey God's commandments (Romans 8:11). But the new believer doesn't become a puppet, and has freedom to disobey God (Galatians 5:16). This is part of the problem today; too many Christians are breaking God's rules too often, and many unbelievers think they're hypocrites and phonies. Christians need to remember that the world is watching them. In Matthew 5:16, Jesus said:

Let your light so shine before men,
that they may see your good works
and glorify you Father in Heaven.

To sum up, believers are not better than unbelievers. The only reason why they will get to enjoy Christ's Kingdom and the Eternal State is because they accepted God's free gift of salvation in Jesus Christ. Sometimes, believers act badly and do things that make unbelievers shake their heads. But being accepted by God doesn't depend on how many good things anybody does. It depends on faith and trust in the Lord Jesus Christ. Unbelievers shouldn't use hypocrites as an excuse not to accept God's free gift; there's an old saying that you have to be smaller than the thing you hide behind. Jesus isn't a phony, and in John 14:6 he said:

I am the way, the truth, and the life.
No one comes to the Father except through me.

If you're not a believer, He waits for you to trust Him (Revelation 3:20). Open the door and let Him in.

Chapter Eight
Watch Out For Fakes

Most supermarkets and bookstores sell magazines and books that contain predictions about the future. The people who make these predictions are called "psychics". Some psychics run commercials or have programs on TV. Millions of people wonder about the future, but instead of going to the Bible, they turn to psychics.

Sometimes these predictions come true. Does that automatically mean God was the source of their information? Scripture tells us something very important in Deuteronomy 18:22:

> *If what a prophet proclaims in the name of the LORD does not take place or come true, that is a message the LORD has not spoken...*

A prophet was a person God chose to speak His message to the people. Sometimes, God told the prophet about something that was going to happen in the future. Deuteronomy 18:22 means that these special messengers were right 100% of the time. If God promised that an event would happen, it would happen! This helped early believers tell who had been sent from God and who was just out to fool them.

Although some of today's psychics are sincere people who believe their "gift" comes from God, they are what the Bible calls "false prophets" (Matthew 24:11). Why? Because not all of the predictions they make about the future come true. For example, a very famous lady psychic once predicted that World War III would break out in 1958. It didn't happen. Even some groups that call themselves "Christian" have made false predictions. One church thought they knew the exact day in which Jesus Christ would return to Earth to set up His Kingdom. They put on white robes, went to a mountaintop, and waited. To their disappointment, Jesus did not come back on that day.

The Bible came directly from God (I Timothy 3:16). Any prediction about the future that goes against scripture does not come from God. The Lord doesn't speak "out of both sides of his mouth". It's impossible for Him to tell a lie (Titus 1:2). He will never say one thing in the Bible, and then whisper something that totally contradicts it into the ear of someone else.

Real messages from God will point people toward His Son:

> *Worship God! For the testimony of Jesus*
> *is the Spirit of prophecy.*
> Revelation 19:10B

"Prophecy" is a message from God about the future. The "testimony of Jesus" includes the following truths that the Bible says about Him:

A. Jesus is God the Son (John 1:1, I John 4:9).

B. Jesus is also man (Matthew 1:25).

Jesus was, is, and always will be, perfect - in other words, sinless. (2 Corinthians 5:21).

D. Jesus died on the cross to make it possible for the entire world to spend eternity in Heaven with God (John 3:14-18).

E. Three days after dying, Jesus rose bodily from the grave (John 20:1-28).

F. Faith and trust in Jesus is the ONLY way to Heaven (John 14:6).

G. Jesus will return bodily to Earth (Matthew 24:30, Acts 1:8).

This is not a complete list of what the Bible says about Jesus (John 21:25). But it does contain some basic, extremely important truths about Christ. Along with making false predictions about the future, another sign that someone is a false prophet is when they contradict what the Bible says about God's Son. And that's even if the person is a minister, preacher, Reverend, Sunday School teacher, or a loyal church goer who carries around a big Bible.

Let's see how easy it might be to get tricked by a false prophet...

EXAMPLE #1 - A famous rock singer announces that he has been "born again". He's joined a church that believes they know the exact date in which Jesus will come back to Earth. He gives up his music career to get ready for the Lord's return.

If a person is looking for a church, should he join the one that this famous rock star has become involved with? The Bible tells us that Jesus is coming back someday, doesn't it?

ANSWER - Yes, scripture does promise the Lord's return, but it also says that no person on Earth knows exactly when Jesus is coming back (Matthew 25:13). The rock singer has gotten involved with a group that ignores part of the Bible, known as a "cult". (No church has perfect understanding of the Bible. But if a group "throws out" something obvious, watch out!)

Anyone looking for a church should avoid this one.

EXAMPLE #2 - a well-known minister has a TV show and has written many popular books. In the sanctuary of his TV church is a big, wooden cross. This man teaches that Hell is here on Earth, and a loving God would never send anyone to suffer in a place of fire. Millions watch his program, and he seems like a nice guy. Is this television preacher one of God's messengers?

ANSWER - No! The Bible tells us that Hell is a real place (Matthew 11:23, 13:42, Luke 16:23, 2 Peter 2:4 and Revelation 14:10). Everyone has a decision to make; do I believe what the Bible says about Hell, or what some men want me to believe about it?

The idea of a place of eternal, fiery punishment is not a pleasant thought. But the Bible is not a book of "wishful thinking"; it's completely honest and "tells it like it is". Reject or ignore this truth about Hell, and you'll end up in a place that you don't think exists.

EXAMPLE #3 - outside of a shopping mall, a lady with a friendly smile hands you a booklet. Inside, it says that Jesus was a very good man and a son of God. Also, it tells you to look within your own spirit and realize that you're just as much a "son of God" as Jesus was. This doesn't sound right, but you can't put your finger on the problem. What does the Bible say about these teachings?

ANSWER - Plenty! Jesus Christ is perfect, and not just "very good" (2 Corinthians 5:21). He is THE Son of God, equal with the Heavenly Father in every way (John 10:30).

To say that Jesus was "A son of God" is to say He was just a sinful human like us (Galatians 3:26). As God's Son, Jesus has power over death (Revelation 1:18). If Jesus is just "A son of God", then believers are trusting a dead man, because there is no way that a mere man has the power to raise himself from the dead! 1 Corinthians 15:17 says:

And if Christ has not been raised, your faith is futile; you are still in your sins.

But Jesus Christ did rise from the dead (Mark 16:6), and believers are trusting a living person who loves and cares for them very much.

THROW THAT BOOKLET AWAY! Go get a Bible, and read what it says about Jesus. An excellent place to start are the first four books of the New Testament, called *the Gospels*. These books paint an accurate picture of Who Jesus Christ is.

Millions of people get fooled every year by false prophets, and many get trapped into false religious groups (cults) because they haven't taken time to read and learn the Bible. People should be on the lookout for fakes; cults like to use verses about the Tribulation, the Rapture, the Second Coming of Jesus and others to scare people into joining their group.

Many of these false teachings are simple to spot, if you just learn some of the basic teachings of scripture. Make an honest effort to study the Bible, and you won't be so easy to fool!

Chapter Nine
Four Amazon Predictions About the Future

The Lord has been amazing people for centuries. Many of the predictions spoken by God's prophets have already happened and are history. Some of these "prophecies" seemed pretty wild when they were first given. But the "almighty" God had the power to make sure they came to pass!

This chapter contains four things God promised would happen hundreds of years BEFORE they actually did. Bible teachers call these totally accurate predictions "fulfilled prophecies". We can't mention every fulfilled prophecy in the Bible, because those would fill a book or two by themselves!

As you read, keep in mind that the same God who made sure these prophecies were fulfilled has promised to fulfill the ones in the Bible about future events like the Rapture, the Tribulation and the Second Coming. Hopefully, when finished, your trust in the Bible will be increased.

AMAZING PROPHECY #1 - the exact name of the town in which God's Son would be born.

But you, Bethlehem Ephrathah, though you are small among the clans of Judah, out of you will come forth to me one who will be ruler over Israel, whose origins are from old, from ancient times.

Micah 5:2

This prophecy was given 800 years BEFORE Jesus was born. And where was Jesus born? Almost everyone is familiar with that part of the Christmas story:

After Jesus was born in Bethlehem in Judea,
during the time of King Herod, Magi from
the east came to Jerusalem.
Matthew 2:1

The Lord promised that His Son would be born in Bethlehem, and that's exactly what happened!

AMAZING PROPHECY #2 - the birth of God's Son would not be caused by sexual relations between a man and a woman.

Therefore the Lord himself will give you a sign;
the virgin will be with child and will give birth to
a son, and will call his name Immanuel.
Isaiah 7:14

The birth of Jesus was different because no human caused it. It was a miracle. The Holy Spirit overshadowed Mary, and through the power of God, she became pregnant. Matthew 1:25 tells us that her husband Joseph had nothing to do with it:

But he had no union with her until she gave birth to a son.
And he gave him the name Jesus.

God chose to do it this way, because if Jesus had come from Joseph and Mary, He would have inherited their

41

ruined, dirty spiritual nature. This would have made Him a sinner, like everyone else on Earth. An absolutely perfect person was needed to die for all the sins of the world, so the perfect God caused Mary to become pregnant.

AMAZING PROPHECY #3 - The Son of God would be rejected by people.

He was despised and rejected by men, a man of sorrows, and familiar with suffering. Like one from whom men hide their faces He was despised and we esteemed him not.
Isaiah 53:3

Jesus Christ came to earth and offered the way to know God and escape an eternity in terrible pain. He came in peace and helped people wherever He went. Jesus healed the sick, fed the hungry, and taught marvelous things about God the Father. You would think that people would gladly accept Him and treat Him kindly. WRONG!

But they cried, saying "Crucify Him! Crucify Him!"
Luke 23:21

Instead of being thankful and accepting Him as God's Son, the people He came to love, killed Him. Talk about unfair! If you ever feel rejected by people, remember Jesus. He did absolutely nothing wrong, but was abandoned by His friends in the time of His greatest trouble (Mark 14:50).

AMAZING PROPHECY #4 - although He would be killed, God's Son would rise from the dead.

...because you will not abandon me to the grave, nor will you let your Holy
One see decay.
Psalm 16:10

Jesus is the "Holy One" spoken of in this verse. All bodies that are buried eventually turn to dust. If someone is cremated, their ashes are put into a container. God's "Holy One" was to be different. According to this prophecy, His body wouldn't stay in the grave long enough to turn to dust.

More importantly, Psalm 16:10 shows that God's Son would rise from the dead. Hundreds of years before it happened, the writer of Psalm 16:10 (King David) was given a vision of Christ's resurrection! This prophecy must have seemed incredible, almost unbelievable, to many of those who read it in the centuries before the birth of Jesus. But Jesus did rise from the dead, and all the other unfulfilled promises in the Bible will come to pass, too (including the strange and unusual ones)!

Some cults believe that Jesus only rose from the dead SPIRITUALLY, and His body stayed in the grave. The Bible teaches that the Lord's body and spirit rose from the dead. Thomas was a follower of Jesus who didn't believe reports that Jesus had risen from the dead. Many of his friends told him it was so, but he replied:

Unless I see in his hands the print of the nails, and put my finger into the
print of the nails, and put my hand into His side, I will not believe.
John 20:25B

Thomas wanted proof! And a few days later, Jesus appeared to him, and said:

"Put your finger here; see my hands.
Reach out your hand and put it in my side.
Stop doubting and believe."
John 20:27B

Thomas discovered that Christ's resurrection wasn't just a spiritual resurrection. Psalm 16:10 was fulfilled just as God promised.

This prophecy is very important, because if Jesus doesn't have power over death, then He is not God. And if He's not God, His body is dust by now, and can't save anyone from anything. But He is alive! In Revelation 1:18, Jesus tells us:

I am the Living One; I was dead, and behold I am alive for ever and ever!
And I hold the keys of death and Hades.

(Hades is another name for Hell).

God keeps His word. He who promised His Son would be born of a virgin, also promises that His Son will return someday to set up a wonderful kingdom. The same God who told his special messengers His "Holy One" would rise from the dead, warns of the coming Rapture, First Resurrection and the Tribulation. He has also told us about a wicked future leader called the Antichrist, the Second Resurrection, the Eternal State and other details of His future plans. He hasn't told us everything (Revelation 10:4), but has revealed enough to keep us all busy studying the Bible for the rest of our lives.

When God says something is going to happen, it will happen!

He is in control!

Bible Reference
Scripture Quotations are from the King James Version

CHAPTER 1

a) Matthew 24:4-22:

4: And Jesus answered and said unto them, Take heed that no man deceive you.

5: For many shall come in My name, saying, I am Christ; and shall deceive many.

6: And ye shall hear of wars and rumours of wars: see that ye be not troubled: for all these things must come to pass, but the end is not yet.

7: For nation shall rise against nation, and kingdom against kingdom: and there shall be famines, and pestilences, and earthquakes, in divers places.

8: All these are the beginning of sorrows.

9: Then shall they deliver you up to be afflicted, and shall kill you: and ye shall be hated of all nations for My name's sake.

10: And then shall many be offended, and shall betray one another, and shall hate one another.

11: And many false prophets shall rise, and shall deceive many.

12: And because iniquity shall abound, the love of many shall wax cold.

13: But he that shall endure unto the end, the same shall be saved.

14: And this gospel of the kingdom shall be preached in all the world for a witness unto all nations; and then shall the end come.

15: When ye therefore shall see the abomination of desolation, spoken of by Daniel the prophet, stand in the holy place, (whoso readeth, let him understand:)

16: Then let them which be in Judaea flee into the mountains:

17: Let him which is on the housetop not come down to take any thing out of his house:

18: Neither let him which is in the field return back to take his clothes.

19: And woe unto them that are with child, and to them that give suck in those days!

20: But pray ye that your flight be not in the winter, neither on the sabbath day:

21: For then shall be great tribulation, such as was not since the beginning of the world to this time, no, nor ever shall be.

22: And except those days should be shortened, there should no flesh be saved: but for the elect's sake those days shall be shortened.

b) Proverbs 2:6:

6: For the LORD giveth wisdom: out of His mouth cometh knowledge and understanding.

Matthew 17:5:

5: While He yet spake, behold, a bright cloud overshadowed them: and behold a voice out of the cloud, which said, This is my beloved Son, in whom I am well pleased; hear ye Him.

Isaiah 9:6:

6: For unto us a child is born, unto us a son is given: and the government shall be upon His shoulder: and His name shall be called Wonderful, Counseller, The Mighty God, The Everlasting Father, The Prince of Peace.

John 1:3:

3: All things were made by Him; and without Him was not any thing made that was made.

Colossian 2:3:

3: In whom are hid all the treasures of wisdom and knowledge.

2 Corinthians 5:21:

21: For He hath made Him to be sin for us, who knew no sin; that we might be made the righteousness of God in Him.

Matthew 8:23-27:

23: And when He was entered into a ship, His disciples followed him.

24: And, behold, there arose a great tempest in the sea, insomuch that the ship was covered with the waves: but He was asleep.

25: And His disciples came to Him, and awoke Him, saying, Lord, save us: we perish.

26: And He saith unto them, Why are ye fearful, O ye of little faith? Then He arose, and rebuked the winds and the sea; and there was a great calm.

27: But the men marvelled, saying, What manner of man is this, that even the winds and the sea obey him!

Matthew 9:1-8:

1: And He entered into a ship, and passed over, and came into His own city.

2: And, behold, they brought to Him a man sick of the palsy, lying on a bed: and Jesus seeing their faith said unto the sick of the palsy; Son, be of good cheer; thy sins be forgiven thee.

3: And, behold, certain of the scribes said within themselves, This man blasphemeth.

4: And Jesus knowing their thoughts said, Wherefore think ye evil in your hearts?

5: For whether is easier, to say, Thy sins be forgiven thee; or to say, Arise, and walk?

6: But that ye may know that the Son of Man hath power on earth to forgive sins, (then saith He to the sick of the palsy,) Arise, take up thy bed, and go unto thine house.

7: And he arose, and departed to his house.

8: But when the multitudes saw it, they marvelled, and glorified God, which had given such power unto men.

Revelation 5:11-14:

11: And I beheld, and I heard the voice of many angels round about the throne and the beasts and the elders: and the number of them was ten thousand times ten thousand, and thousands of thousands;

12: Saying with a loud voice, Worthy is the Lamb that was slain to receive power, and riches, and wisdom, and strength, and honour, and glory, and blessing.

13: And every creature which is in heaven, and on the earth, and under the earth, and such as are in the sea, and all that are in them, heard I saying, Blessing, and honour, and glory, and power, be unto him that sitteth upon the throne, and unto the Lamb for ever and ever.

14: And the four beasts said, Amen. And the four and twenty elders fell down and worshipped Him that liveth for ever and ever.

Exodus 20:3:

3: Thou shalt have no other gods before Me.

John 11:1-54:

1: Now a certain man was sick, named Lazarus, of Bethany, the town of Mary and her sister Martha.

2: (It was that Mary which anointed the Lord with ointment, and wiped His feet with her hair, whose brother Lazarus was sick.)

3: Therefore his sisters sent unto him, saying, Lord, behold, he whom thou lovest is sick.

4: When Jesus heard that, He said, This sickness is not unto death, but for the glory of God, that the Son of God might be glorified thereby.

5: Now Jesus loved Martha, and her sister, and Lazarus.

6: When He had heard therefore that he was sick, He abode two days still in the same place where He was

7: Then after that saith He to His disciples, Let us go into Judaea again.

8: His disciples say unto Him, Master, the Jews of late sought to stone thee; and goest thou thither again?

9: Jesus answered, Are there not twelve hours in the day? If any man walk in the day, he stumbleth not, because he seeth the light of this world.

10: But if a man walk in the night, he stumbleth, because there is no light in him.

11: These things said He: and after that He saith unto them, Our friend Lazarus sleepeth; but I go, that I may awake him out of sleep.

12: Then said His disciples, Lord, if he sleep, he shall do well.

13: Howbeit Jesus spake of his death: but they thought that He had spoken of taking of rest in sleep.

14: Then said Jesus unto them plainly, Lazarus is dead. *15:* And I am glad for your sakes that I was not there, to the intent ye may believe; nevertheless let us go unto him.

16: Then said Thomas, which is called Didymus, unto his fellow disciples, Let us also go, that we may die with Him.

17: Then when Jesus came, He found that he had lain in the grave four days already.

18: Now Bethany was nigh unto Jerusalem, about fifteen furlongs off:

19: And many of the Jews came to Martha and Mary, to comfort them concerning their brother.

20: Then Martha, as soon as she heard that Jesus was coming, went and met Him: but Mary sat still in the house. *21:* Then said Martha unto Jesus, Lord, if thou hadst been here, my brother had not died.

22: But I know, that even now, whatsoever thou wilt ask of God, God will give it thee.

23: Jesus saith unto her, Thy brother shall rise again. *24:* Martha saith unto him, I know that he shall rise again in the resurrection at the last day.

25: Jesus said unto her, I am the resurrection, and the life: he that believeth in me, though he were dead, yet shall he live:

26: And whosoever liveth and believeth in me shall never die. Believest thou this?

27: She saith unto him, Yea, Lord: I believe that thou art the Christ, the Son of God, which should come into the world.

28: And when she had so said, she went her way, and called Mary her sister secretly, saying, The Master is come, and calleth for thee.

29: As soon as she heard that, she arose quickly, and came unto Him.

30: Now Jesus was not yet come into the town, but was in that place where Martha met Him.

31: The Jews then which were with her in the house, and comforted her, when they saw Mary, that she rose up hastily and went out, followed her, saying, She goeth unto the grave to weep there.

32: Then when Mary was come where Jesus was, and saw Him, she fell down at His feet, saying unto Him, Lord, if thou hadst been here, my brother had not died.

33: When Jesus therefore saw her weeping, and the Jews also weeping which came with her, He groaned in the spirit, and was troubled,

34: And said, Where have ye laid him? They said unto Him, Lord, come and see.

35: Jesus wept.

36: Then said the Jews, Behold how He loved him!

37: And some of them said, Could not this man, which opened the eyes of the blind, have caused that even this man should not have died?

38: Jesus therefore again groaning in Himself cometh to the grave. It was a cave, and a stone lay upon it.

39: Jesus said, Take ye away the stone. Martha, the sister of him that was dead, saith unto Him, Lord, by this time he stinketh: for he hath been dead four days.

40: Jesus saith unto her, Said I not unto thee, that, if thou wouldest believe, thou shouldest see the glory of God?

41: Then they took away the stone from the place where the dead was laid. And Jesus lifted up His eyes, and said, Father, I thank thee that thou hast heard Me.

42: And I knew that thou hearest Me always: but because of the people which stand by I said it, that they may believe that thou hast sent Me.

43: And when He thus had spoken, He cried with a loud voice, Lazarus, come forth.

44: And he that was dead came forth, bound hand and foot with graveclothes: and his face was bound about with a napkin. Jesus saith unto them, Loose him, and let him go.

45: Then many of the Jews which came to Mary, and had seen the things which Jesus did, believed on Him.

46: But some of them went their ways to the Pharisees, and told them what things Jesus had done.

47: Then gathered the chief priests and the Pharisees a council, and said, What do we? For this man doeth many miracles.

48: If we let Him thus alone, all men will believe on Him: and the Romans shall come and take away both our place and nation.

49: And one of them, named Caiaphas, being the high priest that same year, said unto them, Ye know nothing at all,

50: Nor consider that it is expedient for us, that one man should die for the people, and that the whole nation perish not.

51: And this spake he not of himself: but being high priest that year, he prophesied that Jesus should die for that nation;

52: And not for that nation only, but that also He should gather together in one the children of God that were scattered abroad.

53: Then from that day forth they took counsel together for to put Him to death.

54: Jesus therefore walked no more openly among the Jews; but went thence unto a country near to the wilderness, into a city called Ephraim, and there continued with His disciples.

Matthew 28:6-7:

6: He is not here: for He is risen, as He said. Come, see the place where the Lord lay.

7: And go quickly, and tell His disciples that He is risen from the dead; and, behold, He goeth before you into Galilee; there shall ye see Him: lo, I have told you.

John 10:30-33:

30: I and My Father are one.

31: Then the Jews took up stones again to stone Him.

32: Jesus answered them, Many good works have I shewed you from My Father; for which of those works do ye stone Me?

33: The Jews answered Him, saying, For a good work we stone thee not; but for blasphemy; and because that thou, being a man, makest thyself God.

Micah 5:2:

2: But thou, Bethlehem Ephratah, though thou be little among the thousands of Judah, yet out of thee shall He come forth unto Me that is to be ruler in Israel; whose goings forth have been from of old, from everlasting.

Hebrews 2:9-10:

9: But we see Jesus, who was made a little lower than the angels for the suffering of death, crowned with glory and honour; that He by the grace of God should taste death for every man.

10: For it became Him, for whom are all things, and by whom are all things, in bringing many sons unto glory, to make the captain of their salvation perfect through sufferings.

John 10:38:

38: But if I do, though ye believe not Me, believe the works: that ye may know, and believe, that the Father is in Me, and I in Him.

Matthew 24:44:

44: Therefore be ye also ready: for in such an hour as ye think not the Son of Man cometh.

CHAPTER 2

Hebrews 9:27:

27: And as it is appointed unto men once to die, but after this the judgment:

John 14:6:

6: Jesus saith unto him, I am the way, the truth, and the life: no man cometh unto the Father, but by Me.

John 3:16:

16: For God so loved the world, that He gave His only begotten Son, that whosoever believeth in Him should not perish, but have everlasting life.

Romans 10:9-10:

9: That if thou shalt confess with thy mouth the Lord Jesus, and shalt believe in thine heart that God hath raised Him from the dead, thou shalt be saved.
10: For with the heart man believeth unto righteousness; and with the mouth confession is made unto salvation.

Mathew 25:41:

41: Then shall He say also unto them on the left hand, Depart from Me, ye cursed, into everlasting fire, prepared for the devil and his angels:

Genesis 7:11:
11: In the six hundredth year of Noah's life, in the second month, the seventeenth day of the month, the same day were all the fountains of the great deep broken up, and the windows of heaven were opened.

Jonah 2:10:
10: And the LORD spake unto the fish, and it vomited out Jonah upon the dry land.

Daniel 6:19-22:
19: Then the king arose very early in the morning, and went in haste unto the den of lions.
20: And when he came to the den, he cried with a lamentable voice unto Daniel: and the king spake and said to Daniel, O Daniel, servant of the living God, is thy God, whom thou servest continually, able to deliver thee from the lions?
21: Then said Daniel unto the king, O king, live for ever.
22: My God hath sent his angel, and hath shut the lions' mouths, that they have not hurt me: forasmuch as before him innocency was found in me; and also before thee, O king, have I done no hurt.

I Thessalonians 4:16:
16: For the Lord himself shall descend from heaven with a shout, with the voice of the archangel, and with the trump of God: and the dead in Christ shall rise first:

I John 3:2:

2: Beloved, now are we the sons of God, and it doth not yet appear what we shall be: but we know that, when He shall appear, we shall be like Him; for we shall see Him as He is.

Revelation 19:7-9:

7: Let us be glad and rejoice, and give honour to Him: for the marriage of the Lamb is come, and His wife hath made herself ready.

8: And to her was granted that she should be arrayed in fine linen, clean and white: for the fine linen is the righteousness of saints.

9: And He saith unto me, Write, Blessed are they which are called unto the marriage supper of the Lamb. And He saith unto me, These are the true sayings of God.

2 Corinthians 9:10:

10: Now he that ministereth seed to the sower both minister bread for your food, and multiply your seed sown, and increase the fruits of your righteousness;

1 Corinthians 3:14-15:

14: If any man's work abide which he hath built thereupon, he shall receive a reward.

15: If any man's work shall be burned, he shall suffer loss: but he himself shall be saved; yet so as by fire.

Ephesians 2:8-10:

8: For by grace are ye saved through faith; and that not of yourselves: it is the gift of God:

9: Not of works, lest any man should boast.

10: For we are his workmanship, created in Christ Jesus unto good works, which God hath before ordained that we should walk in them.

Revelation 4:10:

10: The four and twenty elders fall down before Him that sat on the throne, and worship Him that liveth for ever and ever, and cast their crowns before the throne, saying,

CHAPTER 3

Genesis 17:1:

1: And when Abram was ninety years old and nine, the LORD appeared to Abram, and said unto him, I am the Almighty God; walk before Me, and be thou perfect.

Hebrews 6:18:

18: That by two immutable things, in which it was impossible for God to lie, we might have a strong consolation, who have fled for refuge to lay hold upon the hope set before us

1 John 3:9:

9: Whosoever is born of God doth not commit sin; for His seed remaineth in him: and he cannot sin, because he is born of God.

Revelation 7:9-14:

9: After this I beheld, and, lo, a great multitude, which no man could number, of all nations, and kindreds, and people, and tongues, stood before the throne, and before the Lamb, clothed with white robes, and palms in their hands;
10: And cried with a loud voice, saying, Salvation to our God which sitteth upon the throne, and unto the Lamb.
11: And all the angels stood round about the throne, and about the elders and the four beasts, and fell before the throne on their faces, and worshipped God,
12: Saying, Amen: Blessing, and glory, and wisdom, and thanksgiving, and honour, and power, and might, be unto our God for ever and ever. Amen.

13: And one of the elders answered, saying unto me, What are these which are arrayed in white robes? and whence came they?

14: And I said unto him, Sir, thou knowest. And he said to me, These are they which came out of great tribulation, and have washed their robes, and made them white in the blood of the Lamb.

Matthew 24:21:

21: For then shall be great tribulation, such as was not since the beginning of the world to this time, no, nor ever shall be.

Revelation 16:2-21:

2: And the first went, and poured out his vial upon the earth; and there fell a noisome and grievous sore upon the men which had the mark of the beast, and upon them which worshipped his image.

3: And the second angel poured out his vial upon the sea; and it became as the blood of a dead man: and every living soul died in the sea.

4: And the third angel poured out his vial upon the rivers and fountains of waters; and they became blood.
5: And I heard the angel of the waters say, Thou art righteous, O Lord, which art, and wast, and shalt be, because thou hast judged thus.

6: For they have shed the blood of saints and prophets, and thou hast given them blood to drink; for they are worthy.

7: And I heard another out of the altar say, Even so, Lord God Almighty, true and righteous are thy judgments.

8: And the fourth angel poured out his vial upon the sun; and power was given unto him to scorch men with fire.

9: And men were scorched with great heat, and blasphemed the name of God, which hath power over these plagues: and they repented not to give him glory.

10: And the fifth angel poured out his vial upon the seat of the beast; and his kingdom was full of darkness; and they gnawed their tongues for pain,

11: And blasphemed the God of heaven because of their pains and their sores, and repented not of their deeds.

12: And the sixth angel poured out his vial upon the great river Euphrates; and the water thereof was dried up, that the way of the kings of the east might be prepared.

13: And I saw three unclean spirits like frogs come out of the mouth of the dragon, and out of the mouth of the beast, and out of the mouth of the false prophet.

14: For they are the spirits of devils, working miracles, which go forth unto the kings of the earth and of the whole world, to gather them to the battle of that great day of God Almighty.

15: Behold, I come as a thief. Blessed is he that watcheth, and keepeth his garments, lest he walk naked, and they see his shame.

16: And he gathered them together into a place called in the Hebrew tongue Armageddon.

17: And the seventh angel poured out his vial into the air; and there came a great voice out of the temple of heaven, from the throne, saying, It is done.

18: And there were voices, and thunders, and lightnings; and there was a great earthquake, such as was not since men were upon the earth, so mighty an earthquake, and so great.

19: And the great city was divided into three parts, and the cities of the nations fell: and great Babylon came in remembrance before God, to give unto her the cup of the wine of the fierceness of his wrath.

20: And every island fled away, and the mountains were not found.

21: And there fell upon men a great hail out of heaven, every stone about the weight of a talent: and men blasphemed God because of the plague of the hail; for the plague thereof was exceeding great.

CHAPTER 4

1 John 2:18:

18: Little children, it is the last time: and as ye have heard that antichrist shall come, even now are there many antichrists; whereby we know that it is the last time.

Revelation 13:1:

1: And I stood upon the sand of the sea, and saw a beast rise up out of the sea, having seven heads and ten horns, and upon his horns ten crowns, and upon his heads the name of blasphemy.

Revelation 13:11:

11: And I beheld another beast coming up out of the earth; and he had two horns like a lamb, and he spake as a dragon.

Revelation 13:14:

14: And deceiveth them that dwell on the earth by the means of those miracles which he had power to do in the sight of the beast; saying to them that dwell on the earth, that they should make an image to the beast, which had the wound by a sword, and did live.

Daniel 11:36-37:

36: And the king shall do according to his will; and he shall exalt himself, and magnify himself above every god, and shall speak marvellous things against the God of gods, and shall prosper till the indignation be accomplished: for that that is determined shall be done.

37: Neither shall he regard the God of his fathers, nor the desire of women, nor regard any god: for he shall magnify himself above all.

Revelation 13:4:
4: And they worshipped the dragon which gave power unto the beast: and they worshipped the beast, saying, Who is like unto the beast? Who is able to make war with him?

Revelation 6:8:
8: And I looked, and behold a pale horse: and his name that sat on him was Death, and Hell followed with him. And power was given unto them over the fourth part of the earth, to kill with sword, and with hunger, and with death, and with the beasts of the earth.

Revelation 6:12:
12: And I beheld when he had opened the sixth seal, and, lo, there was a great earthquake; and the sun became black as sackcloth of hair, and the moon became as blood;

Revelation 13:16:
16: And he causeth all, both small and great, rich and poor, free and bond, to receive a mark in their right hand, or in their foreheads:

Revelation 7:14-17:
14: And I said unto him, Sir, thou knowest. And he said to me, These are they which came out of great tribulation, and have washed their robes, and made them white in the blood of the Lamb.

15: Therefore are they before the throne of God, and serve him day and night in his temple: and he that sitteth on the throne shall dwell among them.

16: They shall hunger no more, neither thirst any more; neither shall the sun light on them, nor any heat.

17: For the Lamb which is in the midst of the throne shall feed them, and shall lead them unto living fountains of waters: and God shall wipe away all tears from their eyes

Revelation 13:15:

15: And he had power to give life unto the image of the beast, that the image of the beast should both speak, and cause that as many as would not worship the image of the beast should be killed.

CHAPTER 5

Revelation 1:7:

7: Behold, He cometh with clouds; and every eye shall see Him, and they also which pierced Him: and all kindreds of the earth shall wail because of Him. Even so, Amen.

Revelation 7:9-17:

9: After this I beheld, and, lo, a great multitude, which no man could number, of all nations, and kindreds, and people, and tongues, stood before the throne, and before the Lamb, clothed with white robes, and palms in their hands;
10: And cried with a loud voice, saying, Salvation to our God which sitteth upon the throne, and unto the Lamb.
11: And all the angels stood round about the throne, and about the elders and the four beasts, and fell before the throne on their faces, and worshipped God,
12: Saying, Amen: Blessing, and glory, and wisdom, and thanksgiving, and honour, and power, and might, be unto our God for ever and ever. Amen.
13: And one of the elders answered, saying unto me, What are these which are arrayed in white robes? and whence came they?
14: And I said unto him, Sir, thou knowest. And he said to me, These are they which came out of great tribulation, and have washed their robes, and made them white in the blood of the Lamb.
15: Therefore are they before the throne of God, and serve Him day and night in His temple: and He that sitteth on the throne shall dwell among them.
16: They shall hunger no more, neither thirst any more; neither shall the sun light on them, nor any heat.
17: For the Lamb which is in the midst of the throne shall feed them, and shall lead them unto living fountains of

waters: and God shall wipe away all tears from their eyes.

2 Peter 3:9:

9: The Lord is not slack concerning His promise, as some men count slackness; but is longsuffering to us-ward, not willing that any should perish, but that all should come to repentance.

Romans 10:9-11:

9: That if thou shalt confess with thy mouth the Lord Jesus, and shalt believe in thine heart that God hath raised Him from the dead, thou shalt be saved.

10: For with the heart man believeth unto righteousness; and with the mouth confession is made unto salvation.

11: For the scripture saith, Whosoever believeth on Him shall not be ashamed

Revelation 9:20-21:

20: And the rest of the men which were not killed by these plagues yet repented not of the works of their hands, that they should not worship devils, and idols of gold, and silver, and brass, and stone, and of wood: which neither can see, nor hear, nor walk:

21: Neither repented they of their murders, nor of their sorceries, nor of their fornication, nor of their thefts.

Revelation 11:7:

7: And when they shall have finished their testimony, the beast that ascendeth out of the bottomless pit shall make war against them, and shall overcome them, and kill them.

Revelation 13:16-18:

16: And he causeth all, both small and great, rich and poor, free and bond, to receive a mark in their right hand, or in their foreheads:

17: And that no man might buy or sell, save he that had the mark, or the name of the beast, or the number of his name.

18: Here is wisdom. Let him that hath understanding count the number of the beast: for it is the number of a man; and his number is six hundred threescore and six.

Revelation 1:3:

3: Blessed is he that readeth, and they that hear the words of this prophecy, and keep those things which are written therein: for the time is at hand.

Revelation 22:7:

7: Behold, I come quickly: blessed is he that keepeth the sayings of the prophecy of this book.

Revelation 16:15-17:

15: Behold, I come as a thief. Blessed is he that watcheth, and keepeth his garments, lest he walk naked, and they see his shame.

16: And he gathered them together into a place called in the Hebrew tongue Armageddon.

17: And the seventh angel poured out his vial into the air; and there came a great voice out of the temple of heaven, from the throne, saying, It is done.

Revelation 20:4:

4: And I saw thrones, and they sat upon them, and judgment was given unto them: and I saw the souls of them that were beheaded for the witness of Jesus, and for the word of God, and which had not worshipped the beast, neither his image, neither had received his mark upon their foreheads, or in their hands; and they lived and reigned with Christ a thousand years

Revelation 20:10-15:

10: And the devil that deceived them was cast into the lake of fire and brimstone, where the beast and the false prophet are, and shall be tormented day and night for ever and ever. *11:* And I saw a great white throne, and him that sat on it, from whose face the earth and the heaven fled away; and there was found no place for them.
12: And I saw the dead, small and great, stand before God; and the books were opened: and another book was opened, which is the book of life: and the dead were judged out of those things which were written in the books, according to their works.
13: And the sea gave up the dead which were in it; and death and hell delivered up the dead which were in them: and they were judged every man according to their works.
14: And death and hell were cast into the lake of fire. This is the second death.
15: And whosoever was not found written in the book of life was cast into the lake of fire

Revelation 20:17:

17: And the Spirit and the bride say, Come. And let him that heareth say, Come. And let him that is athirst come. And whosoever will, let him take the water of life freely.

Revelation 3:20:

20: Behold, I stand at the door, and knock: if any man hear My voice, and open the door, I will come in to him, and will sup with him, and he with Me.

Revelation 10:1-4:

1: And I saw another mighty angel come down from heaven, clothed with a cloud: and a rainbow was upon his head, and his face was as it were the sun, and his feet as pillars of fire:

2: And he had in his hand a little book open: and he set his right foot upon the sea, and his left foot on the earth,

3: And cried with a loud voice, as when a lion roareth: and when he had cried, seven thunders uttered their voices.

4: And when the seven thunders had uttered their voices, I was about to write: and I heard a voice from heaven saying unto me, Seal up those things which the seven thunders uttered, and write them not.

Revelation 21:1:

1: And I saw a new heaven and a new earth: for the first heaven and the first earth were passed away; and there was no more sea.

Revelation 19:16:

16: And He hath on His vesture and on His thigh a name written, KING OF KINGS, AND LORD OF LORDS

CHAPTER 6

Isaiah 2:4
4: And He shall judge among the nations, and shall rebuke many people: and they shall beat their swords into plowshares, and their spears into pruninghooks: nation shall not lift up sword against nation, neither shall they learn war any more

b) Isaiah 2:1-3:
1: the word that Isaiah the son of Amoz saw concerning Judah and Jerusalem.
2: And it shall come to pass in the last days, that the mountain of the LORD's house shall be established in the top of the mountains, and shall be exalted above the hills; and all nations shall flow unto it.
3: And many people shall go and say, Come ye, and let us go up to the mountain of the LORD, to the house of the God of Jacob; and He will teach us of His ways, and we will walk in His paths: for out of Zion shall go forth the law, and the word of the LORD from Jerusalem

Isaiah 35:10:
10: And the ransomed of the LORD shall return, and come to Zion with songs and everlasting joy upon their heads: they shall obtain joy and gladness, and sorrow and sighing shall flee away

Micah 4:4:
4: But they shall sit every man under his vine and under his fig tree; and none shall make them afraid: for the mouth of the LORD of hosts hath spoken it

Isaiah 65:20:

20: There shall be no more thence an infant of days, nor an old man that hath not filled his days: for the child shall die an hundred years old; but the sinner being an hundred years old shall be accursed.

Revelation 22:4:

4: And they shall see His face; and His name shall be in their foreheads

Isaiah 11:9:

9: They shall not hurt nor destroy in all My holy mountain: for the earth shall be full of the knowledge of the LORD, as the waters cover the sea

Psalm 72:17:

17: His name shall endure for ever: His name shall be continued as long as the sun: and men shall be blessed in Him: all nations shall call Him blessed

Psalm 2:9:

9: Thou shalt break them with a rod of iron; thou shalt dash them in pieces like a potter's vessel

Revelation 20:7-10:

7: And when the thousand years are expired, Satan shall be loosed out of his prison,

8: And shall go out to deceive the nations which are in the four quarters of the earth, Gog and Magog, to gather them together to battle: the number of whom is as the sand of the sea.

9: And they went up on the breadth of the earth, and compassed the camp of the saints about, and the beloved city: and fire came down from God out of heaven, and devoured them.

10: And the devil that deceived them was cast into the lake of fire and brimstone, where the beast and the false prophet are, and shall be tormented day and night for ever and ever

Revelation 20:11-13:

11: And I saw a great white throne, and Him that sat on it, from whose face the earth and the heaven fled away; and there was found no place for them.

12: And I saw the dead, small and great, stand before God; and the books were opened: and another book was opened, which is the book of life: and the dead were judged out of those things which were written in the books, according to their works.

13: And the sea gave up the dead which were in it; and death and hell delivered up the dead which were in them: and they were judged every man according to their works.

Galatians 3:10-11:

10: For as many as are of the works of the law are under the curse: for it is written, Cursed is every one that continueth not in all things which are written in the book of the law to do them.

11: But that no man is justified by the law in the sight of God, it is evident: for, The just shall live by faith

Revelation 20:15:

15: And whosoever was not found written in the book of life was cast into the lake of fire

Revelation 21:1:

1: And I saw a new heaven and a new earth: for the first heaven and the first earth were passed away; and there was no more sea

Revelation 21:23:

23: And the city had no need of the sun, neither of the moon, to shine in it: for the glory of God did lighten it, and the Lamb is the light thereof

Luke 9:20:

20: He said unto them, But whom say ye that I am? Peter answering said, The Christ of God

Revelation 22:5:

5: And there shall be no night there; and they need no candle, neither light of the sun; for the Lord God giveth them light: and they shall reign for ever and ever

Matthew 25:14-23:

14: For the kingdom of heaven is as a man travelling into a far country, who called his own servants, and delivered unto them his goods.

15: And unto one he gave five talents, to another two, and to another one; to every man according to his several ability; and straightway took his journey.

16: Then he that had received the five talents went and traded with the same, and made them other five talents.

17: And likewise he that had received two, he also gained other two.

18: But he that had received one went and digged in the earth, and hid his lord's money.

19: After a long time the lord of those servants cometh, and reckoneth with them.

20: And so he that had received five talents came and brought other five talents, saying, Lord, thou deliveredst unto me five talents: behold, I have gained beside them five talents more.

21: His lord said unto him, Well done, thou good and faithful servant: thou hast been faithful over a few things, I will make thee ruler over many things: enter thou into the joy of thy lord.

22: He also that had received two talents came and said, Lord, thou deliveredst unto me two talents: behold, I have gained two other talents beside them.

23: His lord said unto him, Well done, good and faithful servant; thou hast been faithful over a few things, I will make thee ruler over many things: enter thou into the joy of thy lord.

Isaiah 65:17-25:

17: For, behold, I create new heavens and a new earth: and the former shall not be remembered, nor come into mind.

18: But be ye glad and rejoice for ever in that which I create: for, behold, I create Jerusalem a rejoicing, and her people a joy.

19: And I will rejoice in Jerusalem, and joy in My people: and the voice of weeping shall be no more heard in her, nor the voice of crying.

20: There shall be no more thence an infant of days, nor an old man that hath not filled his days: for the child shall die an hundred years old; but the sinner being an hundred years old shall be accursed.

21: And they shall build houses, and inhabit them; and they shall plant vineyards, and eat the fruit of them.

22: They shall not build, and another inhabit; they shall not plant, and another eat: for as the days of a tree are the days of my people, and mine elect shall long enjoy the work of their hands.

23: They shall not labour in vain, nor bring forth for trouble; for they are the seed of the blessed of the LORD, and their offspring with them.

24: And it shall come to pass, that before they call, I will answer; and while they are yet speaking, I will hear.

25: The wolf and the lamb shall feed together, and the lion shall eat straw like the bullock: and dust shall be the serpent's meat. They shall not hurt nor destroy in all My holy mountain, saith the LORD

Revelation 22:2-4:

2: In the midst of the street of it, and on either side of the river, was there the tree of life, which bare twelve manner of fruits, and yielded her fruit every month: and the leaves of the tree were for the healing of the nations.

3: And there shall be no more curse: but the throne of God and of the Lamb shall be in it; and His servants shall serve Him:

4: And they shall see His face; and His name shall be in their foreheads

Titus 2:13:

13: Looking for that blessed hope, and the glorious appearing of the great God and our Saviour Jesus Christ;

CHAPTER 7

Genesis 1:27:
27: So God created man in His own image, in the image of God created He him; male and female created He them

Genesis 3:6:
6: And when the woman saw that the tree was good for food, and that it was pleasant to the eyes, and a tree to be desired to make one wise, she took of the fruit thereof, and did eat, and gave also unto her husband with her; and he did eat.

Genesis 2:17:
17: But of the tree of the knowledge of good and evil, thou shalt not eat of it: for in the day that thou eatest thereof thou shalt surely die.

Genesis 3:19:
19: In the sweat of thy face shalt thou eat bread, till thou return unto the ground; for out of it wast thou taken: for dust thou art, and unto dust shalt thou return.

Romans 7:19:
19: For the good that I would I do not: but the evil which I would not, that I do.

Ephesians 2:3:

3: Among whom also we all had our conversation in times past in the lusts of our flesh, fulfilling the desires of the flesh and of the mind; and were by nature the children of wrath, even as others.

Revelation 21:27:

27: And there shall in no wise enter into it any thing that defileth, neither whatsoever worketh abomination, or maketh a lie: but they which are written in the Lamb's book of life

2 Peter 3:9:

9: The Lord is not slack concerning His promise, as some men count slackness; but is longsuffering to us-ward, not willing that any should perish, but that all should come to repentance.

Ephesians 2:8-10:

8: For by grace are ye saved through faith; and that not of yourselves: it is the gift of God:

9: Not of works, lest any man should boast.

10: For we are His workmanship, created in Christ Jesus unto good works, which God hath before ordained that we should walk in them.

2 Corinthians 6:16:

16: And what agreement hath the temple of God with idols? For ye are the temple of the living God; as God hath said, I will dwell in them, and walk in them; and I will be their God, and they shall be My people.

Romans 8:11:

11: But if the Spirit of Him that raised up Jesus from the dead dwell in you, He that raised up Christ from the dead shall also quicken your mortal bodies by His Spirit that dwelleth in you

Galatians 5:16:

16: This I say then, Walk in the Spirit, and ye shall not fulfill the lust of the flesh.

CHAPTER 8

Deuteronomy 18:22:
22: When a prophet speaketh in the name of the LORD, if the thing follow not, nor come to pass, that is the thing which the LORD hath not spoken, but the prophet hath spoken it presumptuously: thou shalt not be afraid of him.

Matthew 24:11:
11: And many false prophets shall rise, and shall deceive many

I Timothy 3:16:
16: And without controversy great is the mystery of godliness: God was manifest in the flesh, justified in the Spirit, seen of angels, preached unto the Gentiles, believed on in the world, received up into glory.

Titus 1:2:
2: In hope of eternal life, which God, that cannot lie, promised before the world began;

John 1:1:
1: In the beginning was the Word, and the Word was with God, and the Word was God

1 John 4:9:
9: In this was manifested the love of God toward us, because that God sent His only begotten Son into the world, that we might live through Him

Matthew 1:25:
25: And knew her not till she had brought forth her firstborn son: and he called his name JESUS

2 Corinthians 5:21:
21: For He hath made Him to be sin for us, who knew no sin; that we might be made the righteousness of God in Him

John 3:14-18:
14: And as Moses lifted up the serpent in the wilderness, even so must the Son of Man be lifted up:
15: That whosoever believeth in Him should not perish, but have eternal life.
16: For God so loved the world, that He gave His only begotten Son, that whosoever believeth in Him should not perish, but have everlasting life.
17: For God sent not His Son into the world to condemn the world; but that the world through Him might be saved.
18: He that believeth on Him is not condemned: but He that believeth not is condemned already, because He hath not believed in the name of the only begotten Son of God.

John 20:1-28:
1: The first day of the week cometh Mary Magdalene early, when it was yet dark, unto the sepulchre, and seeth the stone taken away from the sepulchre.
2: Then she runneth, and cometh to Simon Peter, and to the other disciple, whom Jesus loved, and saith unto them, They have taken away the Lord out of the sepulchre, and we know not where they have laid Him.

3: Peter therefore went forth, and that other disciple, and came to the sepulchre.

4: So they ran both together: and the other disciple did outrun Peter, and came first to the sepulchre.

5: And he stooping down, and looking in, saw the linen clothes lying; yet went he not in.

6: Then cometh Simon Peter following him, and went into the sepulchre, and seeth the linen clothes lie,

7: And the napkin, that was about his head, not lying with the linen clothes, but wrapped together in a place by itself.

8: Then went in also that other disciple, which came first to the sepulchre, and he saw, and believed.

9: For as yet they knew not the scripture, that He must rise again from the dead.

10: Then the disciples went away again unto their own home.

11: But Mary stood without at the sepulchre weeping: and as she wept, she stooped down, and looked into the sepulchre,

12: And seeth two angels in white sitting, the one at the head, and the other at the feet, where the body of Jesus had lain.

13: And they say unto her, Woman, why weepest thou? She saith unto them, Because they have taken away my Lord, and I know not where they have laid Him.

14: And when she had thus said, she turned herself back, and saw Jesus standing, and knew not that it was Jesus.

15: Jesus saith unto her, Woman, why weepest thou? Whom seekest thou? She, supposing Him to be the gardener, saith unto Him, Sir, if thou have borne him hence, tell me where thou hast laid him, and I will take him away.

16: Jesus saith unto her, Mary. She turned herself, and saith unto Him, Rabboni; which is to say, Master.

17: Jesus saith unto her, Touch me not; for I am not yet ascended to My Father: but go to My brethren, and say unto them, I ascend unto My Father, and your Father; and to My God, and your God.

18: Mary Magdalene came and told the disciples that she had seen the Lord, and that He had spoken these things unto her.

19: Then the same day at evening, being the first day of the week, when the doors were shut where the disciples were assembled for fear of the Jews, came Jesus and stood in the midst, and saith unto them, Peace be unto you.

20: And when He had so said, He shewed unto them His hands and His side. Then were the disciples glad, when they saw the Lord.

21: Then said Jesus to them again, Peace be unto you: as My Father hath sent Me, even so send I you.

22: And when He had said this, He breathed on them, and saith unto them, Receive ye the Holy Ghost:

23: Whose soever sins ye remit, they are remitted unto them; and whose soever sins ye retain, they are retained.

24: But Thomas, one of the twelve, called Didymus, was not with them when Jesus came.

25: The other disciples therefore said unto him, We have seen the Lord. But he said unto them, Except I shall see in his hands the print of the nails, and put my finger into the print of the nails, and thrust my hand into his side, I will not believe.

26: And after eight days again His disciples were within, and Thomas with them: then came Jesus, the doors being shut, and stood in the midst, and said, Peace be unto you.

27: Then saith He to Thomas, reach hither thy finger, and behold My hands; and reach hither thy hand, and thrust it into My side: and be not faithless, but believing.

28: And Thomas answered and said unto Him, My Lord and my God.

John 21:25:
25: And there are also many other things which Jesus did, the which, if they should be written every one, I suppose that even the world itself could not contain the books that should be written. Amen.

Matthew 25:13:
13: Watch therefore, for ye know neither the day nor the hour wherein the Son of Man cometh.

Matthew 11:23:
23: And thou, Capernaum, which art exalted unto heaven, shalt be brought down to hell: for if the mighty works, which have been done in thee, had been done in Sodom, it would have remained until this day.

Matthew 13:42:
42: And shall cast them into a furnace of fire: there shall be wailing and gnashing of teeth

Luke Luke 16:23:
23: And in hell he lift up his eyes, being in torments, and seeth Abraham afar off, and Lazarus in his bosom

2 Peter 2:4:
4: For if God spared not the angels that sinned, but cast them down to hell, and delivered them into chains of darkness, to be reserved unto judgment

Revelation 14:10:

10: The same shall drink of the wine of the wrath of God, which is poured out without mixture into the cup of His indignation; and he shall be tormented with fire and brimstone in the presence of the holy angels, and in the presence of the Lamb

2 Corinthians 5:21:

21: For He hath made Him to be sin for us, who knew no sin; that we might be made the righteousness of God in Him

John 10:30:

30: I and My Father are one

Galatians 3:26:

26: For ye are all the children of God by faith in Christ Jesus

Revelation 1:18:

18: I am He that liveth, and was dead; and, behold, I am alive for evermore, Amen; and have the keys of hell and of death

Mark 16:6:

6: And he saith unto them, Be not affrighted: Ye seek Jesus of Nazareth, which was crucified: He is risen; He is not here: behold the place where they laid Him.

CHAPTER 9

Mark 14:50:

50: And they all forsook Him, and fled.

Psalm 16:10:

10: For thou wilt not leave My soul in hell; neither wilt thou suffer thine Holy One to see corruption.

Revelation 10:4:

4: And when the seven thunders had uttered their voices, I was about to write: and I heard a voice from heaven saying unto me, Seal up those things which the seven thunders uttered, and write them not.

Bibliography

Brooks, Keith L. *Great Prophetic Themes*. Chicago, IL: Moody Press, 1962.

Burkett, Larry. *The Coming Economic Earthquake*. Chicago, IL: Moody Press, 1991.

Cumbey, Constance. *The Hidden Dangers of the Rainbow*. Shreveport, LA: Huntington House, 1983.

Dyer, Charles H. *The Rise of Babylon*. Wheaton, IL: Tyndale House, 1991.

Hunt, Dave. *Global Peace and the Rise of the Antichrist*. Eugene, OR: Harvest House, 1990.

Kirban, Salem. *Satan's Mark Exposed*. Huntingdon Valley, PA: Salem Kirban, 1981.

Larson, Bob. *Larson's New Book of Cults*. Wheaton, IL: Tyndale House, 1989.

Lindsey, Hal. *The Late Great Planet Earth*. Grand Rapids, MI: Zondervan, 1977.

Ryrie, Charles C. *The Final Countdown*. Wheaton, IL: Victor, 1982.

Theissen, Henry Clarence and Vernon D. Doerksen. *Lectures in Systematic Theology*.

Grand Rapids, IL: Eerdmans, 1979.

Walvoord, John F. *Jesus Christ our Lord*. Chicago, IL: Moody Press, 1969.

Walvoord, John F. *The Rapture Question*. Grand Rapids, IL: Zondervan, 1957.

You can find ALL our books up at Amazon at:
https://www.amazon.com/shop/writers_exchange

or on our website at:
http://www.writers-exchange.com

JOIN ONE LIST. GET FIVE FREE BOOKS.

Join the Writers Exchange E-Publishing readers' list and *immedaitely* get a
free novel! A new download link to a novel in each of our five main genres
(Romance, Fantasy, Science Fiction, Mystery, and Historical) will hit your inbox
every week!

http://bit.ly/WEE-Newsletter

You'll be kept up to date about our giveaways, new releases, and blog highlights.

About the Author

Chris Williams was born on August 25, 1957 in Bristol, PA and grew up in nearby Levittown, PA. After graduating from Neshaminy High School, he attended Shippensburg State College, Shippensburg, PA from 1975-79 where he majored in Journalism.

Since 1979, he has worked in radio as an announcer with stops at stations in Hanover, PA, Shippensburg, PA, Trenton, NJ, Gettysburg, PA and York, PA.

Chris's writing credits include short stories in *THE DOOR, POWER FOR LIVING, LIVE, STANDARD*, and *RENAISSANCE* to name a few.

In addition, *The HANOVER EVENING SUN*, Hanover, PA has published two interviews he wrote with costars from the film *FRIENDLY PERSUASION* (1956).

Also, London Circle Publishing offered three of his e-books from 1999-2002 and and Moo Press of Warwick, NY published three children's picture books written by Chris about working dogs from 2004-2007.

Chris has a B.A. In Communications from Almeda College, Bosie, ID.

He and his wife of 36 years, Sue, live in York County, PA. He has three grown children, each avid readers.

Also his Writers Exchange author page at:

http://www.writers-exchange.com/Chris-Williams.html

If you enjoyed this author's book, then please place a review up at Amazon and any social media sites you frequent!

If you want to read more about other Non-Fictions books by this publisher, they are listed on the following pages...

Cohesive Story Building
(formerly titled FROM FIRST DRAFT
TO FINISHED NOVEL
{A Writer's Guide to Cohesive Story
Building})
By Karen S. Wiesner

(in ebook AND print!)

Revised, Updated, and Reissued Writing Reference

Second Edition

Without layering, a story is one-dimensional, unbelievable, boring. Layers mean stronger characters, settings, plots, suspense, intrigue, emotions and motivation. Layering also produces cohesion of all elements. Characters must blend naturally with the setting the writer has placed them, just as plot becomes an organic part of character and setting. If a story doesn't work, it could very well be because the elements aren't cohesive. Cohesive Story Building shows how each element hinges on the other two and how to mix them until they fuse irrevocably.

Additionally, Cohesive Story Building carefully explores each of stage of story development from brainstorming and outlining to drafting and revision. From a thorough look at the fundamentals of writing to comprehensive story building techniques, as well as submission guidelines and etiquette, this must-have guide will see writers through the entire novel writing process from start to finish.

Set within the framework of comparing the process of building a house to the process of building a story, Cohesive Story Building gives a solid plan of action from start to finish through in-depth examples and exercises, and leave-no-stone-unturned checklists that will help writers take the plan into their own writing. Features detailed examples from published novels to illustrate story-building principles.

Many who have read Karen Wiesner's reference First Draft in 30 Days, which focuses on in-depth outlining and goal-setting, will find Cohesive Story Building a perfect companion to that book.

Publisher Book Page: http://www.writers-exchange.com/Cohesive-Story-Building.html

Amazon (ebook and print): http://mybook.to/CohesiveStoryBuilding

Bonus! Worksheets, Checklists, and Exercises from COHESIVE STORY BUILDING:

One of the questions I was asked most when the first edition of this book was published by Writer's Digest Books was whether the worksheets, checklists, and exercises were available in a usable format. With this second edition, my new publisher and I are offering a download of all of these that are in a usable format, namely Rich Text Format (RTF), which allows for cross-platform document exchange and which most word processors are able to read or write to. In other words, the file allows you to type right into the document and use it over and over as needed! Additionally, for those who prefer a printed version, a paperback booklet is also available.

Publisher Book Page: http://www.writers-exchange.com/Cohesive-Story-Building-Worksheets.html

Amazon: http://mybook.to/CohesiveWorksheets

Cool Off The Hot Seat! Tips for 'Acing' Your Job Interview
By Rebecca Rothman McCoy

Your interviewer is staring you down from across his desk and the butterflies in your stomach are more active than Hitchcock's *Birds*. Your palms are sweating, your heart is racing, and the worst-case scenario is all you can envision in your future. You *want* this job. You *need* this job. You have to have it...! *Has he noticed my discomfort?* you wonder as you stutter when asked what sets you apart from all the others that have been interviewed before you.

No doubt about it. You're firmly in the hot seat. But careful preparation can help you stay cool, calm, and collected. If you've ever wondered if there was some hidden magical secret that would help you land the job of your dreams, the bad news is, no, not really. But if you're unsure of what to say or do during a job interview and don't know any tricks to set you apart from your competition, then this book is for you!

Written by a staffing industry professional with more than twelve years of interviewing experience, *Cool Off the Hot Seat!* answers all your questions about job interviewing from obtaining the interview to the follow-up afterwards. Here are just a few topics you'll read about:

* Tips on how to research companies you're interested in
* Making a great first impression
* Appropriate clothing and accessories
* Answers for the toughest questions
* What an interviewer is looking for
* The most effective ways to do assertive follow-ups

* Working with recruiters
* Handling media interviews like a pro

This guerrilla guide to interviewing technique has substance without fluff, theory or obscure statistics to wade through. The layout of the book is designed to get you up and running as fast as possible while covering all the important areas you'll need to know in order to nail a successful job interview with all the poise and confidence you need and none of the butterflies!

Publisher Book Page: http://www.writers-exchange.com/Cool-Off-The-Hot-Seat.html

Amazon: http://mybook.to/CoolOff

Five Key Skills
By Alan Strickland

Are you someone who has trouble stringing together a few words in nearly every conversation and your idea of an absolute nightmare is standing in the front of a room and addressing a large gathering? Do you suffer from occasional or frequent bouts of indecision, lack of motivation, the inability to set priorities and a tendency to start new tasks before completing others?

Few are lucky enough to be able to speak easily and confidently, taking command of a hall full of people in various degrees of alertness, or simply finessing a one-on-one discussion into a memorably lively chat. The organized few run their lives like clockwork, finishing everything they embark on. When they decide what they do, they do it and beautiful memories are made.

In easily understandable and practical terms, this book endeavors to improve five key personal skills that may lead to a more fulfilled and balanced life for anyone who suffers from common maladies like social awkwardness and disorganization.

Publisher Book Page: http://www.writers-exchange.com/Five-Key-Skills.html
Amazon: http://mybook.to/FiveKeySkills

Metal Machining Made Easy
By Ian Moore-Morrans

Removing and cutting metal through machining operations traditionally uses lathes, drill presses, and milling machines utilizing a variety of cutting tools. *Metal Machining Made Easy* teaches the basics of metal machining right up to precision machining. Whether you're a beginner, hobbyists or have career interest in metalworking, this must-have edition is loaded with illustrations as well as simple yet practical information that demystifies the rules, formulas and tables involved in this interesting trade.

Publisher Book Page: http://www.writers-exchange.com/Metal-Machining-Made-Easy.html

Amazon: http://mybook.to/MetalMachining

Radically Real! The Quest for Authenticity
By David Weiss

Authenticity is, unfortunately, not much found in the church. As Christians, how do we know for sure we're walking the talk, living the example, being the salt and light we're commanded to be in the Bible? Do nonbelievers see the joy and authenticity in our lives?

Radically Real is a wakeup call to believers to look at the way we live our lives and to return to biblical Christianity. To be Fishers of Men, we must leave judgment on the doorstep. Instead of following legalistic rules, we're charged by Jesus to reach out to those around us about our faith and meet them where they are, just like our Lord did!

Radically Real reminds believers of the high price our Savior paid for us out of His great love, gives guidance in keeping our "swords" sharp by staying in the Word and being the fire that burns brightly with the light of Christ in a dark world in need of the Gospel's message. Christianity isn't a cold, lifeless, *ruthless* set of rules that believers must endure in order to get to Heaven. To be a child of God is to have access to a vibrant, exciting and fulfilling life...if only we leave the middle of the road and make the choice to stand with our transforming Lord.

Publisher Book Page: http://www.writers-exchange.com/Radically-Real.html
Amazon: http://mybook.to/RadicallyReal

Writing Blurbs that Sizzle--And Sell!

Make your book fly off the shelves!

Are you an author who dislikes or dreads trying to write back cover blurbs for your stories, or have you started one and want help making yours sizzle with intrigue and impact?

Would you like to utilize a series blurb but you're not sure where to start in covering all the books in your series in one succinct, powerful paragraph?

Would you like to have a short, punchy version of your blurb that can be used in your marketing and author/series branding?

Are you a publisher with a stable full of books that need blurb overhauls?

Every author knows what a back cover blurb is, but crafting an effectively good one is no easy task. Many writers outright dislike writing them or dread the process because so much is at stake if the blurb fails to engage. A sizzling back cover blurb needs to convince readers they absolutely have to read the story inside the pages...or they'll set the book down without ever opening it. Additionally, a powerful series blurb can sell not just one book but all of them in that set! High-concept blurbs are necessary in every author's marketing to provide intriguing "sound bites" for books and series'.

WRITING BLURBS THAT SIZZLE--AND SELL! will teach writers and publishers:

- The basics of blurb crafting: *When* to write them, *how long* they should be, and the *three types* of blurbs.
- Tips and tricks for crafting blurbs including worksheets and checklists to make the process foolproof.
- Techniques in sizing blurbs for a variety of applications as well covering the timely and viable topic of branding with blurbs.
- Step-by-step, do-it-yourself exercises using published works to help you develop blurb writing, revising, and evaluating skills.

WRITING BLURBS THAT SIZZLE--AND SELL! is the definitive guide on how to craft back cover, series, and high-concept

blurbs!
Publisher Book Page: http://www.writers-exchange.com/Writing-Blurbs-that-Sizzle-and-Sell.html
Amazon: http://mybook.to/WritingBlurbsThatSizzle

Made in the USA
Las Vegas, NV
23 April 2021

21921352R00059